The Bayer Color Atlas of
Hypertension

Volume 1

The Bayer Color Atlas of
Hypertension

Volume 1

Peter F. Semple

The Medical Research Council Blood Pressure Unit
Western Infirmary, Glasgow

and

George B. M. Lindop

University Department of Pathology
Western Infirmary, Glasgow

Bayer

**Pharmaceutical
Division**

Pharmaceutical Division

Bayer Corporation
400 Morgan Lane
West Haven, CT 06516-4175

Dear Doctor:

We are pleased to provide you with the new 3-volume *Bayer Color Atlas of Hypertension* authored by Drs. Peter F. Semple and George B. M. Lindop of the University of Glasgow.

This beautifully-illustrated body of work will provide you with a series of broad-perspective "snapshots" of hypertension to enhance your reference collection.

Replete with more than two dozen illustrations, Volume I focuses on target organs of hypertension and the management of blood pressure. Each volume of the series is self-contained, complete with table of contents, bibliography and index.

As distribution of educational material is further evidence of our long-standing commitment to cardiovascular medicine, we hope you will find this atlas interesting and informative.

Sincerely,

H. Brian Allen, MD, FFPM
Director, Scientific Relations
and Health Care Communications

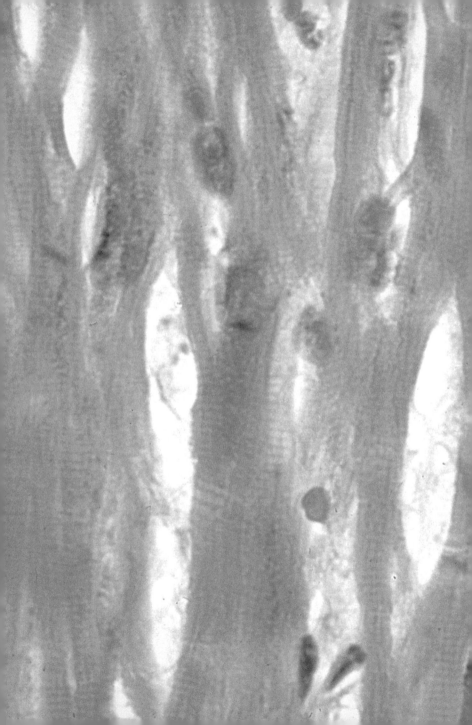

Contents

Introduction

Insurance companies were early to recognize that blood pressure measurements predicted subsequent life expectancy. Numerous epidemiological surveys have established that blood pressure in the population is a continuously distributed variable with a graded relationship to risk of vascular events, so that the definition of 'hypertension' is arbitrary. High blood pressure is closely associated with increased risk of a stroke, a risk that is substantially reduced by treatment with drugs. The correlation between blood pressure and risk of coronary events is not as close as the evidence that this risk is reduced by treatment is less established. The dividing line between 'normal' and 'high' pressures is often set at 160/95 mmHg, which is the level chosen by the World Health Organization. By most common criteria, around 10–20% of adults will develop raised levels of blood pressure in middle life. There is a tendency for people found to have a raised level at routine testing to show lower values if measurements are repeated over weeks or months, and this is thought to reflect both an attenuation of the alarm reaction and a statistical phenomenon known as regression to the mean.

Inherited factors are important in the pathogenesis of the most common form of high blood pressure, which is labelled primary or essential hypertension. The relevant genes have not been identified but there are likely to be several. Environmental factors have also been recognized and include obesity, dietary sodium intake, diabetes mellitus and excessive intake of alcohol. Only about 5% of the hypertensive population have a recognizable cause and this subset is referred to as having 'secondary hypertension'. Such secondary hypertension is often due to underlying renal disease, of which renovascular disease is an important and potentially remediable component. Other less common but well recognized causes include conditions of the adrenal cortex such as primary aldosteronism and of the adrenal medulla and related tissues such as pheochromocytoma.

Untreated severe hypertension may develop into an accelerated or malignant form, which presents with characteristic symptoms and signs. The presence of bilateral flame-shaped retinal hemorrhages is diagnostic. These fundal changes are accompanied by fibrinoid necrosis in the arterioles of the kidney. In the developed world, the incidence of accelerated hypertension seems to be declining, which probably reflects improvements in screening and better treatment with drugs.

The majority of individuals with raised pressure have no symptoms unless a cardiovascular event such as stroke or myocardial infarction has occurred. High blood pressure is one of several factors that accelerate the development of atherosclerosis and result in coronary heart disease. Blood pressure interacts positively with other factors such as blood levels of cholesterol and cigarette smoking. Because treatment trials in hypertension have shown a less clear-cut effect on myocardial infarction when compared to the clear reduction in event rate for stroke and heart failure, there has been a tendency to shift emphasis towards an integrated approach to treatment of all risk factors in the individual patient.

The target organs

Brain

The risk of stroke is directly related to the arterial pressure and this graded relationship seems to be maintained into the normal range of diastolic pressures. A recent meta-analysis of nine prospective observational studies confirmed the view that there is no convincing evidence for a 'threshold' level of diastolic blood pressure at which risk begins. One of the problems in establishing this point is the very low incidence of strokes in individuals with low diastolic blood pressure levels (< 75 mmHg). In general and for increases in sustained diastolic blood pressure of 5, 7.5 and 10 mmHg respectively, there are increases in stroke risk from 34% through 46% to 56%. Of the factors that predict stroke, blood pressure is dominant, although other independent risk factors have been identified, and these include smoking, plasma levels of cholesterol and, perhaps, also of fibrinogen. The incidence of stroke is particularly low in some undeveloped societies where the average diastolic pressure may be only 60 mmHg. In China and Japan, high blood pressure and stroke are common but coronary heart disease is relatively rare: the difference is probably due to marked differences in the prevailing levels of blood cholesterol and low density lipoproteins.

Just over 10% of all clinical strokes are caused by cerebral hemorrhage. Hemorrhages usually develop after rupture of microaneurysms, which develop on the deep penetrating branches of the main cerebral arteries in patients with chronic high blood pressure. Small aneurysms have been identified in arteries 50–200 μm in diameter, mainly at sites of branching and concentrated in lateral branches of the striate arteries and the penetrating arteries of the cortex. The density of lesions is highest in the putamen, globus pallidus, caudate nucleus, thalamus and external capsule. There is now good evidence to link hemorrhage to this type of vascular lesion. Compared to cerebral infarction, the clinical presentation of hemorrhage is usually abrupt with headache, vomiting and impairment of consciousness.

Another common type of lesion associated with uncontrolled hypertension is a small infarct which evolves into a slit-like space or lacuna between 0.5 and 15 mm in diameter and situated deep in the brain. These lesions, which are often undetectable on computed tomography, are caused by occlusion of one of the same small arteries that give rise to hemorrhage. Arteries proximal to lacunae show segmented disorganization of the vessel wall, which results from mechanical disruption of the intima leading to deposition of plasma constituents in the vessel wall. This change, which has been called lipohyalinosis, occurs in regions that are close to high-pressure arteries but not in vessels of the same caliber that are remote from larger arteries. Lacunae may develop at the base of the pons or in cerebellar white matter as well as the subcapsular region. The vulnerability of these small brain arteries to damage has not been clearly explained, but one factor of relevance may be the relative underdevelopment of muscle and elastic tissue layers. It is also possible that intraluminal pressures are higher than in arteries of similar diameter elsewhere, and high pressures may be emphasized by the way that cerebral arteries and arterioles autoregulate flow in response to alterations in perfusion pressure. Another vascular bed which shows tight autoregulation of flow is the renal circulation, also vulnerable to damage in chronic arterial hypertension, and then leading to loss of nephrons.

Lacunar infarcts resulting from small vessel disease probably account for about a quarter of all ischemic strokes, and tend to present as episodes of pure motor hemiparesis, pure sensory deficit or unilateral incoordination. It is characteristic that there is no evidence of cortical dysfunction such as dysphasia, neglect, agnosia or apraxia. A proportion of transient ischemic attacks may result from this type of small vessel disease. It is likely that both hemorrhage and lacunar infarcts are readily prevented by effective treatment of raised arterial pressures.

Most strokes in the hypertensive population are due to atheromatous disease in extracranial vessels, most often arising at the origin of the internal carotid artery in the neck. Plaques of atheroma probably localize at this site because blood flow is turbulent at a point of bifurcation. Internal carotid artery occlusion most often results in cerebral infarction in the distribution of the middle or anterior cerebral arteries or both, and infarcts may become hemorrhagic. Vascular occlusion is usually caused by rupture of a plaque with superimposed thrombosis, but in some instances artery-to-artery embolism of plaque or thrombus may occur. Episodes of transient cerebral ischemia, which tend to be stereotyped in clinical presentation, are usually hemodynamic rather than embolic and caused by severe narrowing (90%) of the internal carotid artery. In narrowed vessels, the velocity of blood flow is increased and this change of velocity in the carotid may be detected using Doppler ultrasound, often used in combination with a two-dimensional image of structures, referred to as the Duplex ultrasound method. Embolic episodes tend to have more variable neurological effects. Transient loss of vision in one eye or amaurosis fugax may result from embolism from a proximal arterial plaque and sometimes the embolus can be visualized as a refractile cholesterol-rich deposit or deposits within the retinal arterioles.

Treatment trials have now shown that drug treatment of hypertension reduces the incidence of fatal and non-fatal stroke by about 40%, and benefit seems to be obtained after quite short periods of blood pressure reduction. The major outcome trials have not differentiated between hemorrhage, small lacunar strokes and large vessel atheromatous events. Antihypertensive drug treatment may be useful in secondary prevention of stroke but particular care is necessary in patients with carotid stenosis due to atherosclerosis. Aspirin is now commonly prescribed for secondary prevention of ischemic strokes, but has the potential to worsen hemorrhagic events. Undue lowering of systemic arterial pressure in a patient with carotid stenosis may provoke an ischemic event.

Retina
A diagnosis of accelerated or malignant hypertension may be established clinically if there are bilateral linear or flame-shaped retinal hemorrhages in association with arterial pressures which are greater than 120 mmHg diastolic. Before there was effective drug treatment for hypertension, around 80% of patients with malignant hypertension died within a year. Affected patients almost invariably have fibrinoid necrosis of arterioles in the kidney. Blurring of vision is a common presenting complaint and other common symptoms are occipital headache, exertional dyspnea and

weight loss. Bleeding events such as epistaxis or hemospermia may also develop. Earlier and more effective treatment has made it rare for patients to develop encephalopathy with obtundation and seizures.

The presence of papilloedema signifies that there is edema of the brain due to raised intracranial pressure, but in itself does not seem to define a group of patients with a prognosis that is much different from those with retinal hemorrhages and 'cotton wool' spots. Hemorrhages in one eye are not sufficient for a diagnosis and may result from a retinal vascular accident such as branch vein occlusion, which also has an increased incidence in hypertensive patients. When hemorrhages and papilloedema are present, 'cotton wool' spots may also be seen in the fundi and are due to areas of infarction of the nerve fiber layer of the retina. In contrast, the so-called 'hard exudate' is caused by escape of plasma from damaged small vessels ultimately leading to refractile deposits with a high lipid content. These lesions tend to cluster at the macula and may give rise to an appearance described as a macular star. Hemorrhages, 'cotton wool' spots and papilloedema resolve within a few weeks of starting effective antihypertensive therapy, but hard exudates may persist for several months.

Hyaline degeneration of the wall of retinal arterioles causes increased light reflection on ophthalmoscopy and develops in response to aging and to high blood pressure. Detection of minor changes is not generally of great value in assessing individuals with raised blood pressure. More severe grades of high blood pressure cause retinal arterioles to resemble silver wires which then appear to nip the retinal veins at crossing points. Such nipping tends to be present if hypertension is more severe or persistent. Decisions about antihypertensive treatment are seldom based on the appearance of the retinal arteries alone.

Patients with high blood pressure have an increased incidence of central retinal artery occlusion, as well as occlusions affecting central and branch retinal veins. The finding of an occlusion of a central artery should prompt examination of the internal carotid artery for evidence of a bruit, or carotid stenosis using Duplex ultrasound.

Heart
Left ventricular hypertrophy
An increase in peripheral vascular resistance is a feature of the established phase of primary hypertension in man. The resultant increase in ventricular work causes concentric hypertrophy of the left ventricle. This change in cardiac geometry tends to normalize wall stresses during systole but may have adverse effects on other aspects of function, especially by reducing compliance of the left ventricle and perhaps by increasing myocardial oxygen demand.

Initially, cardiac function is maintained or even augmented but in the later stages there is progressive dilatation of the left ventricle with a steep decline in performance. Ischemia may be caused by the combined effects of small vessel disease and increases in demand for oxygen from hypertrophied muscle cells. There is usually a relative reduction in capillary density, known as rarefaction and an increase in the diffusion distance. Coronary flow reserve, the difference between the normal flow rate and the flow rate at maximal dilatation, is reduced in the hypertrophied ventricle and there may be relatively greater reductions in flow to the myocardium in the subendocardial zone.

Evidence is accumulating which suggests that severe ventricular hypertrophy in treated hypertensive individuals predisposes to serious ventricular arrhythmias and sudden death. In the Framingham Study, left ventricular hypertrophy has been shown to be an independent risk factor for premature death. Over 12 years of follow-up in Framingham, the mortality of patients with left ventricular hypertrophy, by electrocardiographic criteria, was 16% rising to 60% if there was a concurrent 'strain' pattern.

A component of the fall in compliance of the ventricle in hypertension is related to a deposition of increased collagen and may not be reversible. In hypertensive patients with marked ventricular hypertrophy, the stiff and non-compliant left ventricle may not be adequately filled during diastole and a serious decline in cardiac output may ensue if atrial fibrillation results in loss of the active phase of ventricular filling.

Echocardiography is considerably more sensitive than electrocardiography in detecting ventricular hypertrophy in hypertension, although the value of this investigation in most cases of mild-to-moderate hypertension is not established. Problems can arise in the assessment of athletes who may have ventricular hypertrophy due to training: hypertrophy of this type may give electrocardiographic changes identical to those seen in hypertension but is associated with bradycardia caused by an increase in vagal tone.

Atherosclerosis and coronary artery disease
In Europe and North America, high blood pressure is a major risk factor for coronary heart disease and sudden cardiac death. Like stroke, the relationship between blood pressure and coronary events is probably continuous across

the whole blood pressure distribution, with those in the highest quintile of the distribution having an incidence about five times greater than those in the lowest quintile. The event rate in the lowest part of the distribution is again low and variable between studies, but evidence that there is a threshold for risk or a J-shape to the relationship is not very convincing. High blood pressure seems to accelerate atherosclerosis, a process which is also dependent on blood levels of cholesterol, low density lipoprotein cholesterol and other lipoproteins such as lipoprotein (a), as well as cigarette smoking and diabetes mellitus. In Japan and China, where populations have low cholesterol levels but where hypertension and cigarette smoking are common, the incidence of coronary artery disease is still relatively low, but the stroke mortality rate in China is currently about twice that in the United Kingdom.

In very few of the major trials of drug treatment in hypertension have significant reductions in the incidence of myocardial infarction or coronary events been established and the possible reasons for the discrepancy between stroke and cardiac events have been much debated. Trials in moderate-to-severe hypertension in the 1950s and 1960s clearly showed that drug treatment reduced the incidence of congestive heart failure, which probably reflects the reversal or prevention of left ventricular hypertrophy. The apparent reduction in mortality from cardiac events in the EWPHE study of treatment in elderly hypertensives may also be explained on this basis. Despite these observations, it is surprising that the incidence of congestive heart failure in Framingham does not seem to have declined in an era which saw a great increase in the use of antihypertensive drugs.

Various explanations for the failure to reduce the rate of coronary events have been proposed. For example, it is possible that the time course of the effects of lowering blood pressures on atherosclerosis and small vessel disease may be different. Indeed, most of the treatment trials have been of relatively short duration (about 3–5 years) and terminated at the point where a significant reduction in stroke was attained. In most trials, there was a small reduction in the rate of coronary events but the reduction was not often statistically significant. A meta-analysis of the results of all the major trials in mild-to-moderate hypertension does suggest a significant reduction in coronary event rate of about 14%. There have also been speculations that some anti-hypertensive drug treatments, particularly the thiazide diuretics, fail to reduce coronary risk because of adverse effects on other risk factors such as cholesterol and glucose tolerance; this link remains conjecture. Links between diuretic-induced decreases in serum potassium and cardiac arrhythmias have been established but adverse effects of diuretics on mortality have not been convincingly shown.

Aorta and arteries
Vessels exposed to increased intraluminal pressure develop hypertrophy of the media, which is most evident in small arteries and arterioles. Myocytes in large arteries become polyploid. The increase in wall-to lumen ratio in resistance arterioles magnifies pressor responses to vasoconstrictor stimuli. Arteriosclerosis which develops in large and small arteries is a feature of aging and is accelerated in the presence of hypertension. Smooth muscle in the media is replaced by collagen. Small vessels in some vascular beds are particularly prone to develop sclerotic changes and

these include the arteries of the kidney, retina and brain. It is not established that blood flow under normal conditions is compromised by these structural changes but flow reserve is probably reduced. Intimal thickening and reduplication of the internal elastic lamina develop in medium-sized arteries exposed to high intraluminal pressures.

In the 'Windkessel' vessels such as the aorta and other large arteries, there is dilatation, lengthening and loss of compliance. Unfolding and dilatation of the ascending aorta may be evident on a plain chest radiograph, although the clinical value of such a radiograph in uncomplicated hypertension is not well established. The loss of elasticity of large arteries is responsible for the relatively greater increase of systolic rather than of diastolic pressure with age. It is not clear if this isolated systolic hypertension of the elderly should be treated with drugs, although an increased risk of vascular events in affected individuals is well established. Severe hypertension also causes an increase in glycosaminoglycan deposition in the media of the aorta, which predisposes to dissection. Aortic dissection is an infrequent but well recognized complication of chronic hypertension.

Kidneys

Renal failure often develops in patients with malignant hypertension, but is now relatively uncommon in less severe grades of hypertension, perhaps due to the effectiveness of antihypertensive drugs. In the era before drugs, early death from renal failure in malignant hypertension was common. The main pathological finding in the kidney in malignant hypertension is fibrinoid necrosis of small arteries and arterioles, which tends to be most prominent in afferent glomerular arterioles but also affects small inter-lobular arteries. The appearance of fibrin in the vessel wall probably results from increased permeability and damage to the endothelium, which allows plasma proteins and fibrino-gen to gain access to the media. There is accompanying necrosis of the smooth muscle cells and thrombosis of the lumen, which results in loss of glomeruli and the appear-ance of red cells and red cell casts in the urine. Another arterial lesion in malignant hypertension is proliferative endarteritis, which is most prominent in the interlobular arteries, leads to a characteristic 'onion skin' appearance and may represent a healing response to endothelial injury.

Widespread fibrin deposition in vessels may cause frag-mentation of circulating red blood cells, resulting in so-called microangiopathic hemolytic anemia. The blood count usually shows moderate thrombocytopenia. Glomeruli undergo focal necrosis, and glomerular capilla-ries may rupture into Bowman's space and the renal tubules, to give hemorrhages, visible to the naked eye as 'flea-bites' on the surface of the kidney. Prognosis in malig-nant hypertension is now related to the degree of impair-ment of renal function rather than to the height of the untreated arterial pressure. In rare instances, untreated malignant hypertension leads to acute renal failure, which is reversed by antihypertensive treatment, but in most instances the damage to renal function caused by malignant hypertension is permanent. Chronic impairment of kidney function is now relatively unusual in treated benign hyper-tension, unless there is underlying primary kidney disease or unless atheromatous renal arterial disease has developed.

Adequate treatment of raised arterial pressure in most forms of chronic renal disease is thought to reduce the rate of deterioration of renal function. This is particularly relevant in patients with autosomal dominant adult polycystic kidney disease, in whom hypertension may be an early feature and where there is an associated risk of intracranial berry aneurysms (10–40%).

A rise in renovascular resistance is an early feature of most forms of clinical and experimental hypertension, but does not necessarily lead to glomerular injury. In untreated moderate-to-severe hypertension, there is a progressive reduction in renal plasma flow with an increase in filtration fraction, leading to maintenance of the glomerular filtration rate until a relatively late stage. Thereafter, glomerular sclerosis and nephron loss lead to a progressive reduction in glomerular filtration rate with hyperfiltration in residual nephrons, which become increased in size. Brenner has proposed that the increase in capillary pressure from overperfusion of residual nephrons is the pathogenetic mechanism that causes progressive loss of nephrons and progression of renal failure.

In insulin-dependent diabetes mellitus, high blood pressure is an early feature in patients destined to develop clinical nephropathy and renal failure. Antihypertensive therapy has been shown to reduce protein excretion in early diabetic nephropathy, although it has yet to be shown that such early treatment reduces the incidence of clinical nephropathy. Converting enzyme inhibitors, which do not have an adverse metabolic effect on diabetes, are undergoing long-term clinical trials at present. Antihypertensive treatment in patients with established nephropathy, as in most forms of kidney disease, also seems to slow the decline of glomerular filtration rate.

Hypertension illustrated

List of illustrations

Figure 1 A coronal section of brain showing a recent cerebral hematoma, centered on the basal ganglia. In 1889 Charcot and Bouchard discovered 'miliary' aneurysms on the small penetrating arteries after microscopic examination of brain tissue that had been squashed between glass slides

Figure 2 Another consequence of uncontrolled hypertension is hemorrhage into cerebellum (in this instance, the right lobe). Common presenting symptoms are vomiting, loss of balance, vertigo and occipital headache

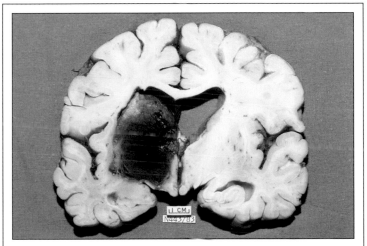

Figure 1

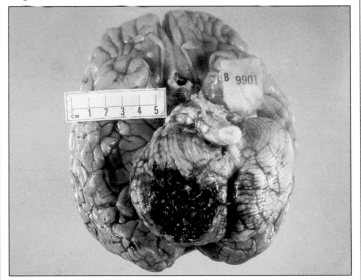

Figure 2

Figure 3 Intracerebral hematoma in a hypertensive patient shown by computed tomography. The lesion is centered on the internal capsule and there is a surrounding zone of edema leading to compression of the anterior horn of the ventricle. In uncontrolled hypertension, hemorrhage of this type results from rupture of microaneurysms which develops on penetrating arteries deep in the brain

Figure 4 A coronal section of brain with an established infarct in the distribution of the middle cerebral artery. Lesions of this type most often result from thrombosis on atheromatous plaques in the extracranial carotid system

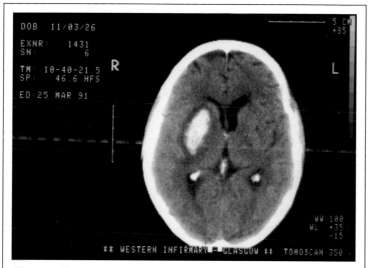

Figure 3

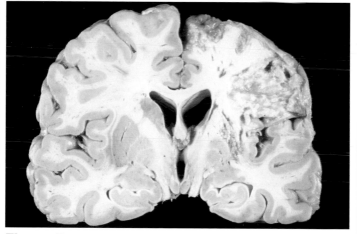

Figure 4

Figure 5 The pons is another common site for hemorrhage in uncontrolled hypertension. Coma develops early after such an event

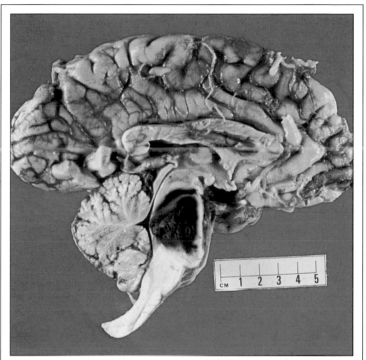

Figure 5

Figure 6 Computed tomographic scan showing small bilateral areas of reduced attenuation deep to the internal capsules in a patient with poorly controlled hypertension. These 'lacunar' infarcts are small (usually <1.5 cm diameter), occur in the distribution of the same small penetrating arteries that rupture to produce cerebral hemorrhage and may not be visualized by CT

Figure 7 A computed tomographic scan showing a hypodense area consistent with a previous infarction in the left parietal lobe, in the territory of the middle cerebral artery

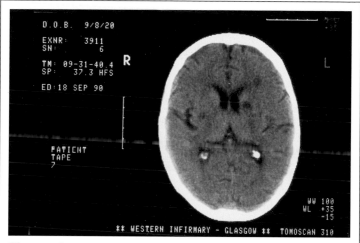

Figure 6

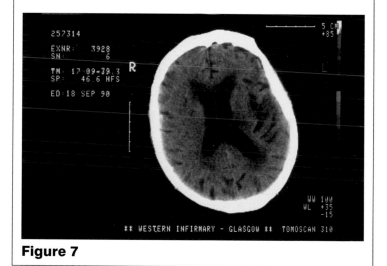

Figure 7

Figure 8 The bifurcation of a carotid artery. There is considerable atheroma in the internal carotid artery and the artery is occluded by thrombus distally

Figure 9 Single photon emission computed tomographic (SPECT) scan showing an axial cut of the brain in a patient with an extensive right hemisphere infarct due to occlusion of the internal carotid artery. Rates of blood flow: red > yellow > green > blue

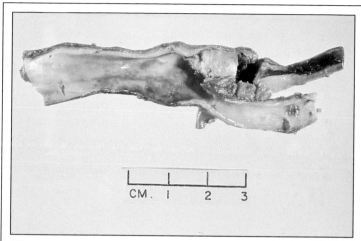

Figure 8

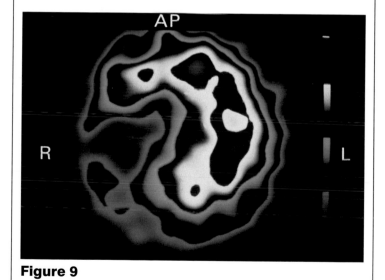

Figure 9

Figure 10 Magnetic resonance image of the brain in a T_1 weighted mode showing generalized edema in a patient with malignant hypertension. The edema is most evident in the posterior fossa and is causing a degree of herniation of the cerebellar tonsils through the foramen magnum

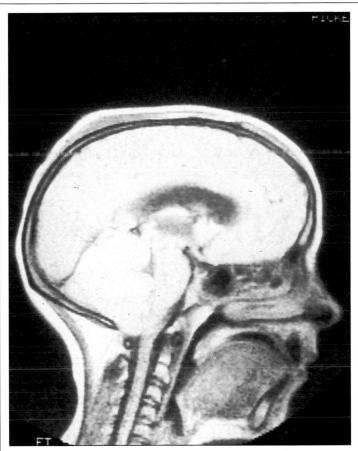

Figure 10

Figure 11 Appearance of the optic fundus in a patient with malignant hypertension. There are linear or flame-shaped retinal hemorrhages and papilloedema. For a clinical diagnosis of malignant hypertension, hemorrhages must be present in both eyes

Figure 12 The retina in malignant hypertension with papilloedema and very prominent hard exudates, described as a macular star

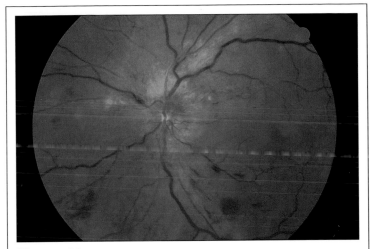

Figure 11

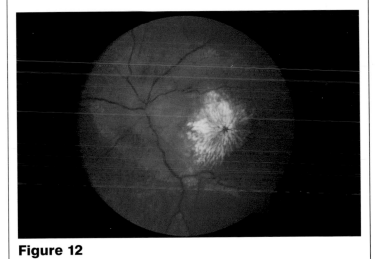

Figure 12

Figure 13 Retinal appearances in a patient with severe hypertension that is not in the malignant phase, showing scattered exudates at the macula

Figure 14 Background retinopathy in a patient with diabetes mellitus. There are dot-and-blot hemorrhages but no evidence of new vessel formation. Hypertension accelerates microvascular disease in diabetes. Obesity, insulin resistance and hypertension often co-exist

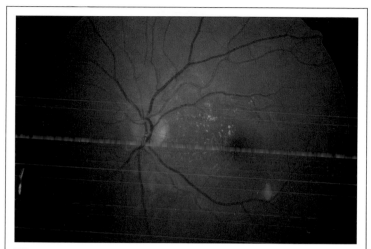

Figure 13

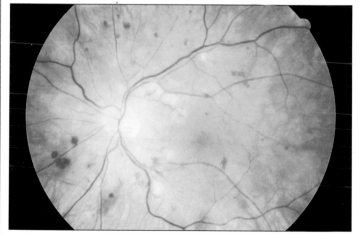

Figure 14

Figure 15 Electrocardiograph from a patient with severe hypertension, showing evidence of left ventricular hypertrophy (LVH) by limb lead and chest lead voltage criteria. There is ST segment depression in the lateral leads which is described as a 'strain' pattern. The usual chest lead criteria for LVH are S wave in Vl + R wave in V5 > 35 mm. For the limb leads, R wave in Vl + S wave in V3 > 25 mm or R wave in lead 1 > 12 mm

Figure 16 To the right is a normal heart and to the left is a heart from a patient with high blood pressure showing an increase in the size and thickness of the left ventricle

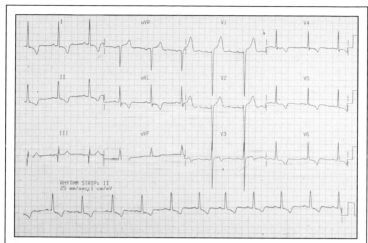

Figure 15

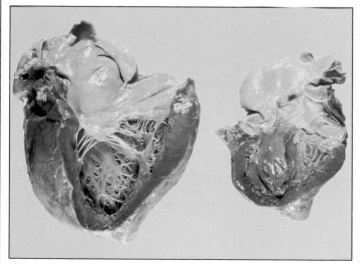

Figure 16

Figure 17 The histological appearances of hypertrophied cardiac myocytes in hypertension (upper panel) contrasted with those of slightly atrophic myocytes of an elderly person (lower panel). The diffusion distance between the lumen of the capillary and the center of the hypertrophied myocyte is increased, which may make the cells susceptible to ischemia. The hypertrophied wall is also stiffer, which results in impairment of ventricular filling

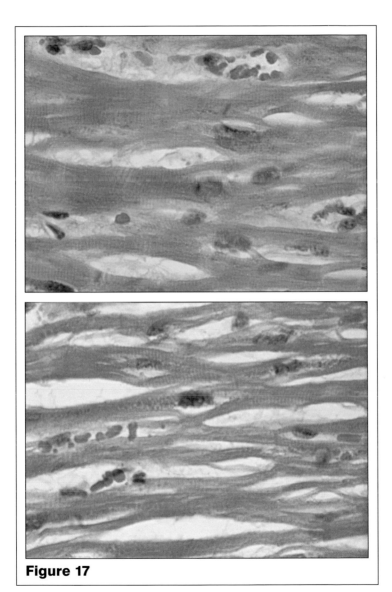

Figure 17

Figure 18 The middle section shows a short burst of ventricular tachycardia in a 24-hour electrocardiograph recording from a patient who had left ventricular hypertrophy due to hypertension. Ventricular hypertrophy in hypertension may be an independent risk factor for cardiovascular events. In treated hypertensive patients there is an association between hypertrophy, ventricular arrhythmias and sudden death

Figure 19 An obese patient with hypertension and left ventricular hypertrophy. Because of the increased thickness of the chest wall, evidence of ventricular hypertrophy is seen only in the limb leads (see also Figure 15)

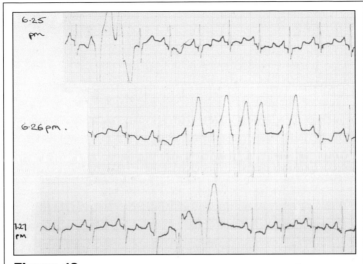

Figure 18

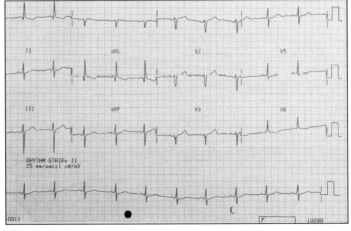

Figure 19

Figure 20 Echocardiography is more sensitive than electrocardiography in detecting left ventricular hypertrophy in hypertension. This is a two-dimensional echocardiogram in the long axis of the heart, showing concentric hypertrophy of the left ventricle with increased thickness of both the interventricular septum and posterior wall (normal 12 mm or less). The aorta is somewhat dilated as a result of stretching of the wall caused by arteriosclerosis

Figure 21 Transesophageal echocardiography is a relatively non-invasive method of detecting aortic dissection although angiography may still be required in some cases. This two-dimensional view of the aorta from the same patient clearly shows a flap and tear. The false lumen is to the left and probably contains some thrombus. Color Doppler demonstrated lower velocities of blood flow in the false lumen compared to the true lumen

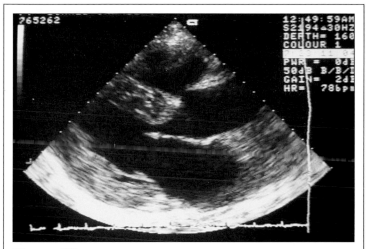

Figure 20

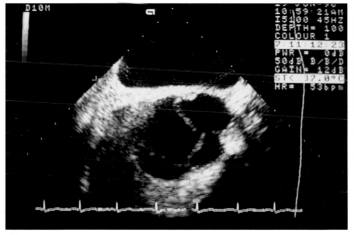

Figure 21

Figure 22 An angiogram of the left coronary artery and its anterior descending (to the right) and circumflex branches (in the center) in a right anterior oblique projection. There is retrograde filling of the distal part of the occluded right coronary artery (below left) from well-developed collaterals. In clinical trials, drug treatment of hypertension has had a disappointing impact on the incidence of coronary events

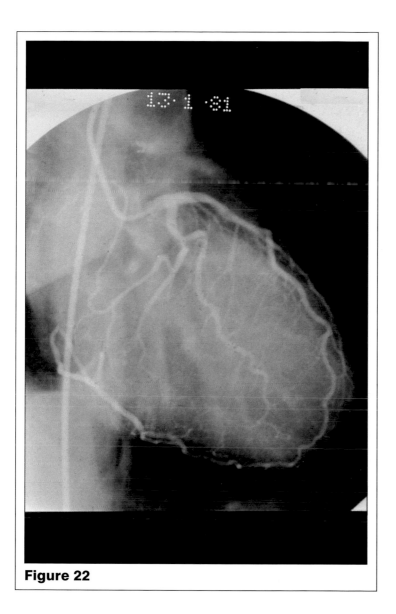

Figure 22

Figure 23 The upper panel shows a recent thrombus at the origin of the right coronary artery close to the aorta. The lower panel shows a histological section through a severely atheromatous coronary artery. The residual media is deep pink in color. The artery is narrowed by atheromatous plaque containing a mixture of pale fibrous tissue and clear lipid material. The cap of the plaque has ruptured, causing hemorrhage into the substance and thrombosis of the lumen

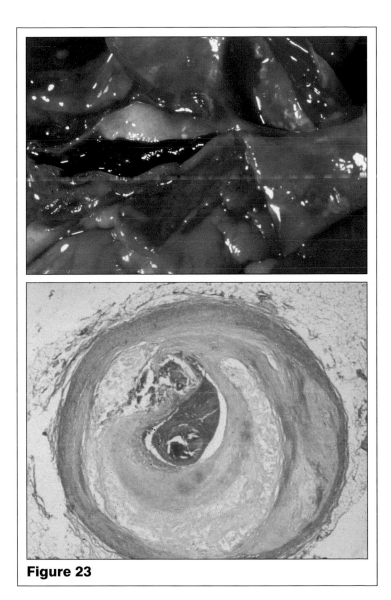

Figure 23

Figure 24 A transverse section through a hypertrophied heart. There is myocardial infarction involving the posterior and septal walls of the left ventricle. The necrotic myocardium is creamy yellow in color and is surrounded by a darker zone of granulation tissue, indicating an infarct of approximately 2 weeks' duration. The coronary arteries on the epicardium are narrowed and yellow due to atheroma

Figure 25 A rare complication of chronic hypertension is aortic dissection. A chest radiograph shows widening of the upper mediastinum caused by blood in the wall of the aorta. In contrast to myocardial infarction, hypertension after the event is characteristic. Pressure should be controlled by intravenous infusion of labetalol or sodium nitroprusside before definitive surgery

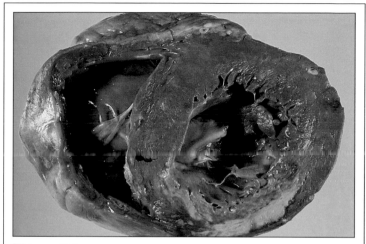

Figure 24

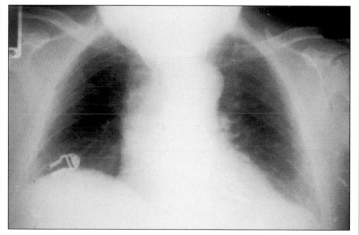

Figure 25

Figure 26 A typical transverse tear (2.5 cm) on the inner aspect of the aorta about 3 cm above the aortic valve. This is the site of initiation of aortic dissection in about 60% of cases. Hematoma is seen around the inner layer of the vessel. Hypertension is the commonest factor that predisposes to aortic dissection

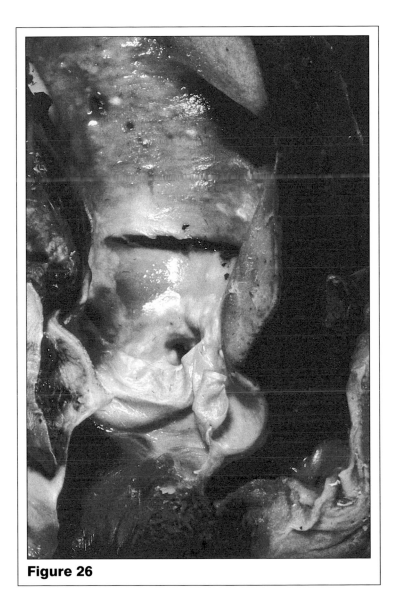

Figure 26

Figure 27 The upper panel shows a low-power section through the aorta of a young woman who died after an aortic dissection. Collagen is stained magenta and elastic laminae are stained black. In the media of the vessel, the elastic laminae are fragmented and there is patchy loss of elastic tissue and smooth muscle. The lower panel shows a high-power view of one of these areas stained with the PAS/alcian blue technique. The spaces in the media are filled by lakes of proteoglycans

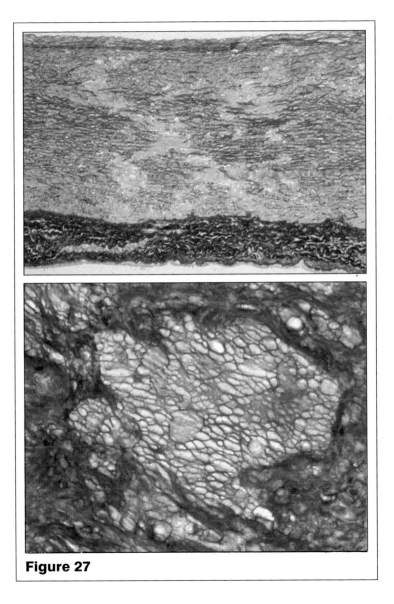

Figure 27

Figure 28 Typical appearance of the kidney in long-standing benign hypertension. The surface is finely granular and the kidney is reduced in size. Similar changes occur in old age

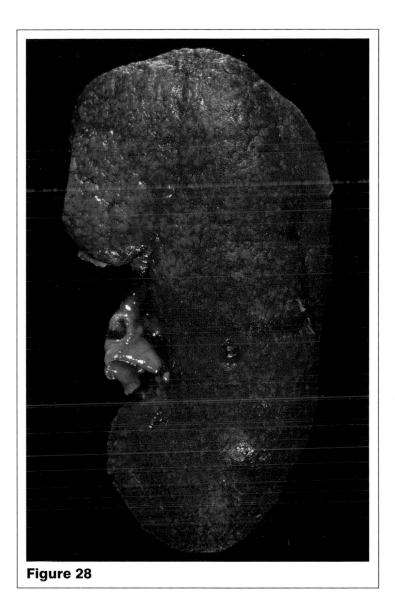

Figure 28

Figure 29 A photomicrograph of the same kidney as in Figure 28 reveals that the granularity is due to small scars, caused by loss of nephrons, interspersed with areas of tubular hypertrophy in residual nephrons

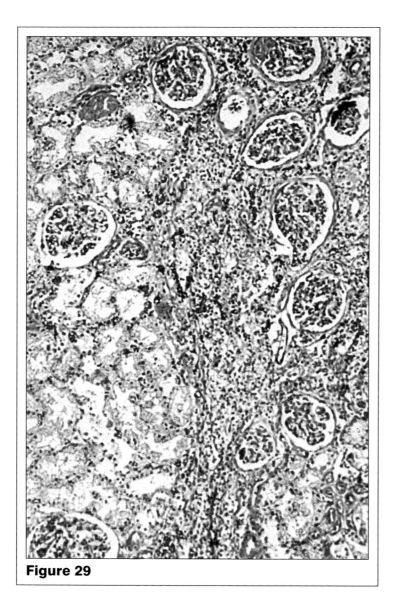

Figure 29

Acknowledgements

Drs Patricia Morley, Andrew Morris, Henry Dargie, James McLenachan, Jehoida Brown, John Connell, Andrew Collier, John Kingdom, Ian More, Amir Azmy and Mr Gerard Hillen all contributed slides and the authors thank them.

modest elevations of LDH and CPK, but normal SGOT. Vital signs remained stable, no electrocardiographic abnormalities were noted and renal function returned to normal within 24 to 48 hours with routine supportive measures alone. No prolonged sequelae were observed.

The effect of a single 900 mg ingestion of nifedipine capsules in a depressed anginal patient on tricyclic antidepressants was loss of consciousness within 30 minutes of ingestion, and profound hypotension, which responded to calcium infusion, pressor agents, and fluid replacement. A variety of ECG abnormalities were seen in this patient with a history of bundle branch block, including sinus bradycardia and varying degrees of AV block. These dictated the prophylactic placement of a temporary ventricular pacemaker, but otherwise resolved spontaneously. Significant hyperglycemia was seen initially in this patient, but plasma glucose levels rapidly normalized without further treatment.

A young hypertensive patient with advanced renal failure ingested 280 mg of nifedipine capsules at one time, with resulting marked hypotension responding to calcium infusion and fluids. No AV conduction abnormalities, arrhythmias, or pronounced changes in heart rate were noted, nor was there any further deterioration in renal function.

DOSAGE AND ADMINISTRATION

Dosage should be adjusted according to each patient's needs. It is recommended that ADALAT CC be administered orally once daily on an empty stomach. ADALAT CC is an extended release dosage form and tablets should be swallowed whole, not bitten or divided. In general, titration should proceed over a 7-14 day period starting with 30 mg once daily. Upward titration should be based on therapeutic efficacy and safety. The usual maintenance dose is 30 mg to 60 mg once daily. Titration to doses above 90 mg daily is not recommended.

If discontinuation of ADALAT CC is necessary, sound clinical practice suggests that the dosage should be decreased gradually with close physician supervision.

Care should be taken when dispensing ADALAT CC to assure that the extended release dosage form has been prescribed.

HOW SUPPLIED

ADALAT CC extended release tablets are supplied as 30 mg, 60 mg, and 90 mg round film coated tablets. The different strengths can be identified as follows:

Strength	Color	Markings
30 mg	Pink	30 on one side and ADALAT CC on the other side
60 mg	Salmon	60 on one side and ADALAT CC on the other side
90 mg	Dark Red	90 on one side and ADALAT CC on the other side

ADALAT® CC Tablets are supplied in:

	Strength	NDC Code
Bottles of 100	30 mg	0026-8841-51
	60 mg	0026-8851-51
	90 mg	0026-8861-51
Unit Dose Packages of 100	30 mg	0026-8841-48
	60 mg	0026-8851-48
	90 mg	0026-8861-48

The tablets should be protected from light and moisture and stored below 86°F (30°C). Dispense in tight, light-resistant containers.

Bayer

Pharmaceutical Division

Distributed by:
Bayer Corporation
Pharmaceutical Division
400 Morgan Lane
West Haven, CT 06516 USA
Made in Germany

There are no adequate and well-controlled studies in pregnant women. ADALAT CC should be used during pregnancy only if the potential benefit justifies the potential risk to the fetus.

Nursing Mothers: Nifedipine is excreted in human milk. Therefore, a decision should be made to discontinue nursing or to discontinue the drug, taking into account the importance of the drug to the mother.

ADVERSE EXPERIENCES

The incidence of adverse events during treatment with ADALAT CC in doses up to 90 mg daily were derived from multi-center placebo-controlled clinical trials in 370 hypertensive patients. Atenolol 50 mg once daily was used concomitantly in 187 of the 370 patients on ADALAT CC and in 64 of the 126 patients on placebo. All adverse events reported during ADALAT CC therapy were tabulated independently of their causal relationship to medication.

The most common adverse event reported with ADALAT® CC was peripheral edema. This was dose related and the frequency was 18% on ADALAT CC 30 mg daily, 22% on ADALAT CC 60 mg daily and 29% on ADALAT CC 90 mg daily versus 10% on placebo.

Other common adverse events reported in the above placebo-controlled trials include:

	ADALAT CC (%) (n=370)	PLACEBO (%) (n=126)
Adverse Event		
Headache	19	13
Flushing/heat sensation	4	0
Dizziness	4	2
Fatigue/asthenia	4	4
Nausea	2	1
Constipation	1	0

Where the frequency of adverse events with ADALAT CC and placebo is similar, causal relationship cannot be established.

The following adverse events were reported with an incidence of 3% or less in daily doses up to 90 mg:

Body as a Whole/Systemic: chest pain, leg pain

Central Nervous System: paresthesia, vertigo

Dermatologic: rash

Gastrointestinal: constipation

Musculoskeletal: leg cramps

Respiratory: epistaxis, rhinitis

Urogenital: impotence, urinary frequency

Other adverse events reported with an incidence of less than 1.0% were:

Body as a Whole/Systemic: cellulitis, chills, facial edema, neck pain, pelvic pain, pain

Cardiovascular: atrial fibrillation, bradycardia, cardiac arrest, extrasystole, hypotension, palpitations, phlebitis, postural hypotension, tachycardia, cutaneous angiectases

Central Nervous System: anxiety, confusion, decreased libido, depression, hypertonia, insomnia, somnolence

Dermatologic: pruritus, sweating

Gastrointestinal: abdominal pain, diarrhea, dry mouth, dyspepsia, esophagitis, flatulence, gastrointestinal hemorrhage, vomiting

Hematologic: lymphadenopathy

Metabolic: gout, weight loss

Musculoskeletal: arthralgia, arthritis, myalgia

Respiratory: dyspnea, increased cough, rales, pharyngitis

Special Senses: abnormal vision, amblyopia, conjunctivitis, diplopia, tinnitus

Urogenital/Reproductive: kidney calculus, nocturia, breast engorgement

The following adverse events have been reported rarely in patients given nifedipine in other formulations: allergenic hepatitis, alopecia, anemia, arthritis with ANA (+), depression, erythromelalgia, exfoliative dermatitis, fever, gingival hyperplasia, gynecomastia, leukopenia, mood changes, muscle cramps, nervousness, paranoid syndrome, purpura, shakiness, sleep disturbances, syncope, taste perversion, thrombocytopenia, transient blindness at the peak plasma level, tremor and urticaria.

OVERDOSAGE

Experience with nifedipine overdosage is limited. Generally, overdosage with nifedipine leading to pronounced hypotension calls for active cardiovascular support including monitoring of cardiovascular and respiratory function, elevation of extremities, judicious use of calcium infusion, pressor agents and fluids. Clearance of nifedipine would be expected to be prolonged in patients with impaired liver function. Since nifedipine is highly protein bound, dialysis is not likely to be of any benefit; however, plasmapheresis may be beneficial.

There has been one reported case of massive overdosage with tablets of another extended release formulation of nifedipine. The main effects of ingestion of approximately 4800 mg of nifedipine in a young man attempting suicide as a result of cocaine-induced depression was initial dizziness, palpitations, flushing, and nervousness. Within several hours of ingestion, nausea, vomiting, and generalized edema developed. No significant hypotension was apparent at presentation, 18 hours post ingestion. Blood chemistry abnormalities consisted of a mild, transient elevation of serum creatinine, and

Beta-Blocker Withdrawal: When discontinuing a beta-blocker it is important to taper its dose, if possible, rather than stopping abruptly before beginning nifedipine. Patients recently withdrawn from beta blockers may develop a withdrawal syndrome with increased angina, probably related to increased sensitivity to catecholamines. Initiation of nifedipine treatment will not prevent this occurrence and on occasion has been reported to increase it.

Congestive Heart Failure: Rarely, patients (usually while receiving a beta-blocker) have developed heart failure after beginning nifedipine. Patients with tight aortic stenosis may be at greater risk for such an event, as the unloading effect of nifedipine would be expected to be of less benefit to these patients, owing to their fixed impedance to flow across the aortic valve.

PRECAUTIONS

General - Hypotension: Because nifedipine decreases peripheral vascular resistance, careful monitoring of blood pressure during the initial administration and titration of ADALAT CC is suggested. Close observation is especially recommended for patients already taking medications that are known to lower blood pressure (See WARNINGS).

Peripheral Edema: Mild to moderate peripheral edema occurs in a dose-dependent manner with ADALAT CC. The placebo subtracted rate is approximately 8% at 30 mg, 12% at 60 mg and 19% at 90 mg daily. This edema is a localized phenomenon, thought to be associated with vasodilation of dependent arterioles and small blood vessels and not due to left ventricular dysfunction or generalized fluid retention. With patients whose hypertension is complicated by congestive heart failure, care should be taken to differentiate this peripheral edema from the effects of increasing left ventricular dysfunction.

Information for Patients: ADALAT CC is an extended release tablet and should be swallowed whole and taken on an empty stomach. It should not be administered with food. Do not chew, divide or crush tablets.

Laboratory Tests: Rare, usually transient, but occasionally significant elevations of enzymes such as alkaline phosphatase, CPK, LDH, SGOT, and SGPT have been noted. The relationship to nifedipine therapy is uncertain in most cases, but probable in some. These laboratory abnormalities have rarely been associated with clinical symptoms; however, cholestasis with or without jaundice has been reported. A small increase (<5%) in mean alkaline phosphatase was noted in patients treated with ADALAT CC. This was an isolated finding and it rarely resulted in values which fell outside the normal range. Rare instances of allergic hepatitis have been reported with nifedipine treatment. In controlled studies, ADALAT CC did not adversely affect serum uric acid, glucose, cholesterol or potassium.

Nifedipine, like other calcium channel blockers, decreases platelet aggregation *in vitro*. Limited clinical studies have demonstrated a moderate but statistically significant decrease in platelet aggregation and increase in bleeding time in some nifedipine patients. This is thought to be a function of inhibition of calcium transport across the platelet membrane. No clinical significance for these findings has been demonstrated.

Positive direct Coombs' test with or without hemolytic anemia has been reported but a causal relationship between nifedipine administration and positivity of this laboratory test, including hemolysis, could not be determined.

Although nifedipine has been used safely in patients with renal dysfunction and has been reported to exert a beneficial effect in certain cases, rare reversible elevations in BUN and serum creatinine have been reported in patients with pre-existing chronic renal insufficiency. The relationship to nifedipine therapy is uncertain in most cases but probable in some.

Drug Interactions: Beta-adrenergic blocking agents: (See WARNINGS).

ADALAT CC was well tolerated when administered in combination with a beta blocker in 187 hypertensive patients in a placebo-controlled clinical trial. However, there have been occasional literature reports suggesting that the combination of nifedipine and beta-adrenergic blocking drugs may increase the likelihood of congestive heart failure, severe hypotension, or exacerbation of angina in patients with cardiovascular disease.

Digitalis. Since there have been isolated reports of patients with elevated digoxin levels, and there is a possible interaction between digoxin and ADALAT CC, it is recommended that digoxin levels be monitored when initiating, adjusting, and discontinuing ADALAT CC to avoid possible over- or under-digitalization.

Coumarin Anticoagulants: There have been rare reports of increased prothrombin time in patients taking coumarin anticoagulants to whom nifedipine was administered. However, the relationship to nifedipine therapy is uncertain.

Quinidine: There have been rare reports of an interaction between quinidine and nifedipine (with a decreased plasma level of quinidine).

Cimetidine: Both the peak plasma level of nifedipine and the AUC may increase in the presence of cimetidine. Ranitidine produces smaller non-significant increases. This effect of cimetidine may be mediated by its known inhibition of hepatic cytochrome P-450, the enzyme system probably responsible for the first-pass metabolism of nifedipine. If nifedipine therapy is initiated in a patient currently receiving cimetidine, cautious titration is advised.

Carcinogenesis, Mutagenesis, Impairment of Fertility: Nifedipine was administered orally to rats for two years and was not shown to be carcinogenic. When given to rats prior to mating, nifedipine caused reduced fertility at a dose approximately 30 times the maximum recommended human dose. *In vivo* mutagenicity studies were negative.

Pregnancy: Pregnancy Category C. In rodents, rabbits and monkeys, nifedipine has been shown to have a variety of embryotoxic, placentotoxic and fetotoxic effects, including stunted fetuses (rats, mice and rabbits), digital anomalies (rats and rabbits), rib deformities (mice), cleft palate (mice), small placentas and underdeveloped chorionic villi (monkeys), embryonic and fetal deaths (rats, mice and rabbits), prolonged pregnancy (rats; not evaluated in other species), and decreased neonatal survival (rats; not evaluated in other species). On a mg/kg or mg/m² basis, some of the doses associated with these various effects are higher than the maximum recommended human dose and some are lower, but all are within an order of magnitude of it.

The digital anomalies seen in nifedipine-exposed rabbit pups are strikingly similar to those seen in pups exposed to phenytoin, and these are in turn similar to the phalangeal deformities that are the most common malformation seen in human children with *in utero* exposure to phenytoin.

No studies have been performed with ADALAT CC in patients with renal failure; however, significant alterations in the pharmacokinetics of nifedipine immediate release capsules have not been reported in patients undergoing hemodialysis or chronic ambulatory peritoneal dialysis. Since the absorption of nifedipine from ADALAT CC could be modified by renal disease, caution should be exercised in treating such patients.

Because hepatic biotransformation is the predominant route for the disposition of nifedipine, its pharmacokinetics may be altered in patients with chronic liver disease. ADALAT CC has not been studied in patients with hepatic disease; however, in patients with hepatic impairment (liver cirrhosis) nifedipine has a longer elimination half-life and higher bioavailability than in healthy volunteers.

The degree of protein binding of nifedipine is high (92%-98%). Protein binding may be greatly reduced in patients with renal or hepatic impairment.

After administration of ADALAT CC to healthy elderly men and women (age > 60 years), the mean C_{max} is 36% higher and the average plasma concentration is 70% greater than in younger patients.

Clinical Studies: ADALAT CC produced dose-related decreases in systolic and diastolic blood pressure as demonstrated in two double-blind, randomized, placebo-controlled trials in which over 350 patients were treated with ADALAT CC 30, 60 or 90mg once daily for 6 weeks. In the first study, ADALAT CC was given as monotherapy and in the second study, ADALAT CC was added to a beta-blocker in patients not controlled on a beta-blocker alone. The mean trough (24 hours post-dose) blood pressure results from these studies are shown below:

MEAN REDUCTIONS IN TROUGH SUPINE BLOOD PRESSURE (mmHg)
SYSTOLIC/DIASTOLIC

ADALAT CC DOSE	STUDY 1 N	MEAN TROUGH REDUCTION*
30 MG	60	5.3/2.9
60 MG	57	8.0/4.1
90 MG	55	12.5/8.1

ADALAT CC DOSE	STUDY 2 N	MEAN TROUGH REDUCTION*
30 MG	58	7.6/3.8
60 MG	63	10.1/5.3
90 MG	62	10.2/5.8

*Placebo response subtracted.

The trough/peak ratios estimated from 24 hour blood pressure monitoring ranged from 41%-78% for diastolic and 46%-91% for systolic blood pressure.

Hemodynamics: Like other slow-channel blockers, nifedipine exerts a negative inotropic effect on isolated myocardial tissue. This is rarely, if ever, seen in intact animals or man, probably because of reflex responses to its vasodilating effects. In man, nifedipine decreases peripheral vascular resistance which leads to a fall in systolic and diastolic pressures, usually minimal in normotensive volunteers (less than 5-10 mm Hg systolic), but sometimes larger. With ADALAT CC, these decreases in blood pressure are not accompanied by any significant change in heart rate. Hemodynamic studies of the immediate release nifedipine formulation in patients with normal ventricular function have generally found a small increase in cardiac index without major effects on ejection fraction, left ventricular end-diastolic pressure (LVEDP) or volume (LVEDV). In patients with impaired ventricular function, most acute studies have shown some increase in ejection fraction and reduction in left ventricular filling pressure.

Electrophysiologic Effects: Although, like other members of its class, nifedipine causes a slight depression of sinoatrial node function and atrioventricular conduction in isolated myocardial preparations, such effects have not been seen in studies in intact animals or in man. In formal electrophysiologic studies, predominantly in patients with normal conduction systems, nifedipine administered as the immediate release capsule has had no tendency to prolong atrioventricular conduction or sinus node recovery time, or to slow sinus rate.

INDICATION AND USAGE

ADALAT CC is indicated for the treatment of hypertension. It may be used alone or in combination with other antihypertensive agents.

CONTRAINDICATIONS

Known hypersensitivity to nifedipine.

WARNINGS

Excessive Hypotension: Although in most patients the hypotensive effect of nifedipine is modest and well tolerated, occasional patients have had excessive and poorly tolerated hypotension. These responses have usually occurred during initial titration or at the time of subsequent upward dosage adjustment, and may be more likely in patients using concomitant beta-blockers.

Severe hypotension and/or increased fluid volume requirements have been reported in patients who received immediate release capsules together with a beta-blocking agent and who underwent coronary artery bypass surgery using high dose fentanyl anesthesia. The interaction with high dose fentanyl appears to be due to the combination of nifedipine and a beta-blocker, but the possibility that it may occur with nifedipine alone, with low doses of fentanyl, in other surgical procedures, or with other narcotic analgesics cannot be ruled out. In nifedipine-treated patients where surgery using high dose fentanyl anesthesia is contemplated, the physician should be aware of these potential problems and, if the patient's condition permits, sufficient time (at least 36 hours) should be allowed for nifedipine to be washed out of the body prior to surgery.

Increased Angina and/or Myocardial Infarction: Rarely, patients, particularly those who have severe obstructive coronary artery disease, have developed well documented increased frequency, duration and/or severity of angina or acute myocardial infarction upon starting nifedipine or at the time of dosage increase. The mechanism of this effect is not established.

Selected bibliography

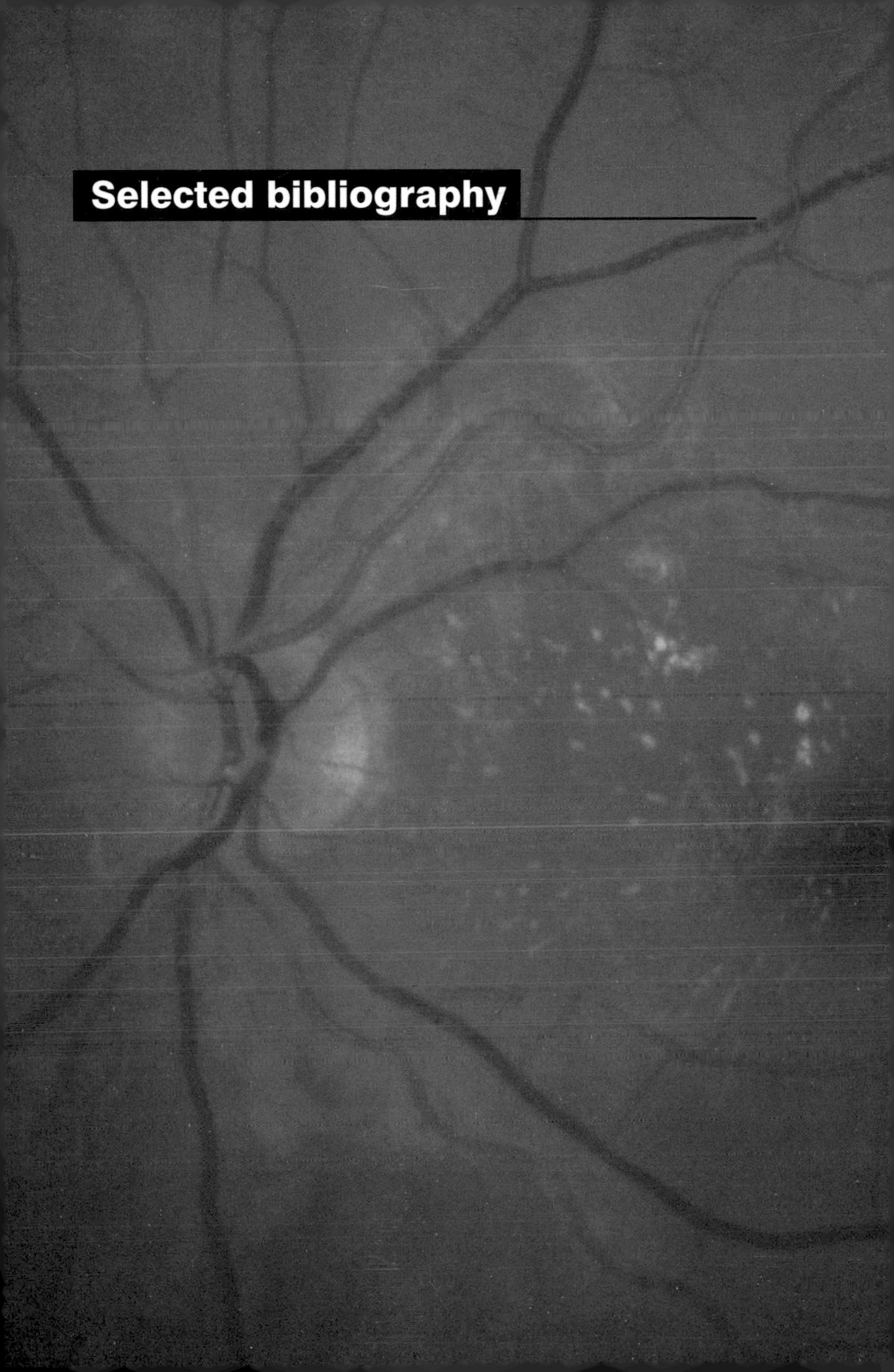

Introduction

Metropolitan Life Insurance Company (1961). *Blood Pressure Insurance Experience and its Implications.* (New York: M. L. I. C.)

Hawthorne, V. M., Greaves, D. A. and Beevers, D. G. (1974). Blood pressure in a Scottish town. *Br. J. Med.*, 3, 600–3

MacMahon, S., Peto, R., Cutler, J., Collins, R., Sorlie, P., Neaton, J., Abbott, R., Godwin, J., Dyer, A. and Stamler, J. (1990). Blood pressure, stroke and coronary heart disease. I. *Lancet*, 335, 765–74

Collins, R., Peto, R., MacMahon, S. Hebert, P., Fiebach, N. H., Eberlein, K. A., Godwin, J., Qizilbash, N., Taylor, J. O. and Hennekens, C. H. (1990). Blood pressure, stroke and coronary heart disease. II. *Lancet*, 335, 827–38

Medical Research Council Working Party (1985). MRC trial of treatment of mild hypertension: principal results. *Br. Med. J.*, 291, 97–104

Report of the British Hypertension Society Working Party (1989). Treating mild hypertension. *Br. Med. J.*, 298, 694–8

Medical Research Council Working Party on Mild Hypertension (1986). Course of blood pressure in mild hypertensives after withdrawal of long term antihypertensive treatment. *Br. Med. J.*, 293, 988–92

United Kingdom prospective diabetes study (1985). Prevalence of hypertension and hypotensive therapy in patients with newly diagnosed diabetes: a multicenter study. *Hypertension*, 7 (Suppl. II), II 8–13

The target organs

Brain

Ramsay, L. E. and Waller, P. C. (1986). Strokes in mild hypertension: diastolic rules. *Lancet*, 2, 854–6

Ross-Russell, R. W. (1963). Observations on intracerebral aneurysms. *Brain*, 86, 425–42

Fisher, C. M. (1969). The arterial lesions underlying lacunes. *Acta Neurol. Pathol.* (Berlin), 12, 1–15

Bamford, J. M., Sandercock, P. A. G., Jones, L. N. and Warlow, C. P. (1987). The natural history of lacunar infarction: the Oxfordshire Community Stroke Project. *Stroke*, 18, 545–51

Hankey, G. J. and Warlow, C. P. (1991). Lacunar transient ischaemic attacks: a clinically useful concept? *Lancet*, 337, 335–8

WHO Task Force on Stroke and Cerebrovascular Disorders (1989). Stroke 89: recommendations on stroke prevention, diagnosis and therapy. *Stroke*, 20, 1407–31

Kase, C. S. (1988). Middle cerebral artery syndromes. In Vinkin, P. J., Bruyn, G. W., Klawans, H. L. and Toole, J. F.

(eds.) *Handbook of Clinical Neurology*, pp. 335–70. (Amsterdam: Elsevier)

MacMahon, S., Peto, S., Cutler, J., Collins, R., Sorlie, P., Neaton, J., Abbott, R., Godwin, J., Dyer, A. and Stamler, J. (1990). Blood pressure, stroke and coronary heart disease. I. *Lancet*, **335**, 765–74

Collins, R., Peto, R., MacMahon, S., Hebert, P., Fiebach, N. H., Eberlein, K. A., Graham, J., Qizilbash, N., Taylor, J. O. and Hennekens, C. H. (1990). Blood pressure, stroke and coronary heart disease. II. *Lancet*, **335**, 827–38

Retina

MacGregor, E., Isles, C. G., Jay, J. L., Lever, A. F. and Murray, G. D. (1986). Retinal changes in malignant hypertension. *Br. Med. J.*, **292**, 233–4

Skinhoj, E. and Strandgaard, S. (1973). Pathogenesis of hypertensive encephalopathy. *Lancet*, **1**, 461–2

Left ventricular hypertrophy

Kannel, W. B., Gordon, T. and Offutt, D. (1969). Left ventricular hypertrophy by electrocardiogram. *Ann. Intern. Med.*, **71**, 98–105

Hammond, I. W., Devereux, R. B., Alderman, M. H., Lutas, E. M., Spitzer, M. C., Crawley, J. S. and Laragh, J. H. (1986). The prevalence and correlates of echocardiographic left ventricular hypertrophy among employed patients with uncomplicated hypertension. *J. Am. Coll. Cardiol.*, **7**, 639–50

Nichols, A. B., Sciacca, R. R., Weiss, M. B., Blood, D. K., Brennan, D. L. and Cannon, P. J. (1980). Effect of left ventricular hypertrophy on myocardial blood flow and ventricular performance in systemic hypertension. *Circulation*, **62**, 329–40

Amery, A., Birkenhager, W., Brixho, P., Bulpitt, C. *et al.* (1985). Mortality and morbidity results from the European working party on high blood pressure in the elderly trial. *Lancet*, **1**, 1349–54

Atherosclerosis and coronary artery disease

MacMahon, S., Peto, R., Cutler, J. Collins, R., Sorlie, P., Neaton, J., Abbott, R., Godwin, J., Dyer, A. and Stamler, J. (1990). Blood pressure, stroke and coronary heart disease. I. *Lancet*, **335**, 765–74

Collins, R., Peto, R., MacMahon, S., Hebert, P., Fiebach, N. H., Eberlein, K. A., Godwin, J., Qizilbash, N., Taylor, J. O. and Hennekens, C. H. (1990). Blood pressure, stroke and coronary heart disease. II. *Lancet*, **335**, 827–38

Lichenstein, M. J., Shipley, M. J. and Rose, G. (1985). Systolic and diastolic blood pressures as predictors of coronary heart disease mortality in the Whitehall study. *Br. Med. J.*, **291**, 243–5

Kidneys

Kincaid-Smith, P., McMichael, J. and Murphy, E. A. (1958). The clinical course and pathology of hypertension with papilloedema (malignant hypertension). *Q. J. Med.*, **27**, 117–53

Breckenbridge, A., Dollery, C. T. and Parry, E. H. O. (1970). Prognosis of treated hypertension. Changes in life expectancy and causes of death between 1952 and 1967. *Q. J. Med.*, 39, 411–29

Van Hooft, I. M. S., Grobbee, D. E., Derkx, F. H. M., De Leeuw, P. W., Schalekamp, M. A. D. H. and Hofman, A. (1991). Renal haemodynamics and the renin–angiotensin–aldosterone system in normotensive subjects with hypertensive and normotensive parents. *N. Engl. J. Med.*, **324**, 1305–11

Mogensen, C. E. and Christensen, C. K. (1984). Predicting diabetic nephropathy in insulin-dependent patients. *N. Engl. J. Med.*, **311**, 89–93

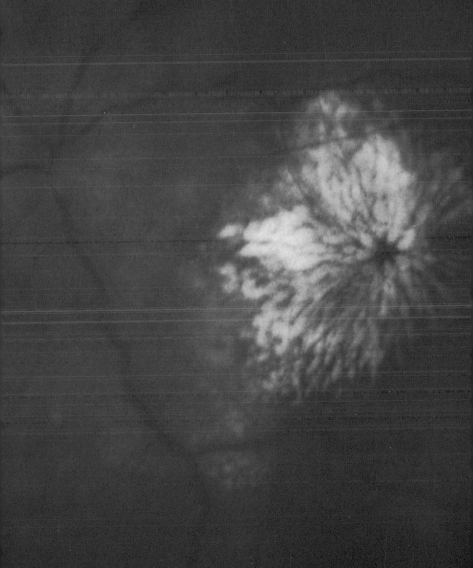

Index

Index

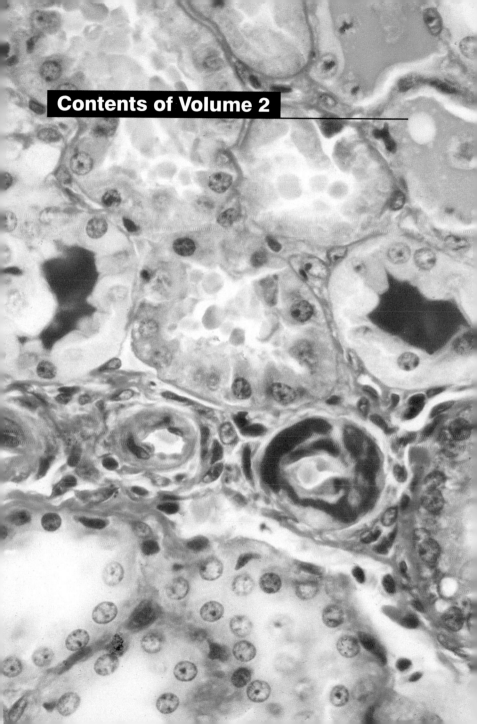

Contents of Volume 2

Contents of Volume 2

List of illustrations in Volume 2

Contents of Volume 3

Contents of Volume 3

List of illustrations in Volume 3

Notes

Notes

Notes

Notes

Notes

Notes

Notes

ADALAT® CC
(nifedipine)
Extended Release Tablets
For Oral Use

PZ500005

DESCRIPTION

ADALAT® CC is an extended release tablet dosage form of the calcium channel blocker nifedipine. Nifedipine is 3,5-pyridinedicarboxylic acid, 1,4-dihydro-2,6-dimethyl-4-(2-nitrophenyl)-dimethyl ester, $C_{17}H_{18}N_2O_6$, and has the structural formula:

Nifedipine is a yellow crystalline substance, practically insoluble in water but soluble in ethanol. It has a molecular weight of 346.3. ADALAT CC tablets consist of an external coat and an internal core. Both contain nifedipine, the coat as a slow release formulation and the core as a fast release formulation. ADALAT CC tablets contain either 30, 60, or 90 mg of nifedipine for once-a-day oral administration.

Inert ingredients in the formulation are: hydroxypropylcellulose, lactose, corn starch, crospovidone, microcrystalline cellulose, silicon dioxide, and magnesium stearate. The inert ingredients in the film coating are: hydroxypropylmethylcellulose, polyethylene glycol, ferric oxide, and titanium dioxide.

CLINICAL PHARMACOLOGY

Nifedipine is a calcium ion influx inhibitor (slow-channel blocker or calcium ion antagonist) which inhibits the transmembrane influx of calcium ions into vascular smooth muscle and cardiac muscle. The contractile processes of vascular smooth muscle and cardiac muscle are dependent upon the movement of extracellular calcium ions into these cells through specific ion channels. Nifedipine selectively inhibits calcium ion influx across the cell membrane of vascular smooth muscle and cardiac muscle without altering serum calcium concentrations.

Mechanism of Action: The mechanism by which nifedipine reduces arterial blood pressure involves peripheral arterial vasodilatation and consequently, a reduction in peripheral vascular resistance. The increased peripheral vascular resistance that is an underlying cause of hypertension results from an increase in active tension in the vascular smooth muscle. Studies have demonstrated that the increase in active tension reflects an increase in cytosolic free calcium.

Nifedipine is a peripheral arterial vasodilator which acts directly on vascular smooth muscle. The binding of nifedipine to voltage-dependent and possibly receptor-operated channels in vascular smooth muscle results in an inhibition of calcium influx through these channels. Stores of intracellular calcium in vascular smooth muscle are limited and thus dependent upon the influx of extracellular calcium for contraction to occur. The reduction in calcium influx by nifedipine causes arterial vasodilation and decreased peripheral vascular resistance which results in reduced arterial blood pressure.

Pharmacokinetics and Metabolism: Nifedipine is completely absorbed after oral administration. The bioavailability of nifedipine as ADALAT CC relative to immediate release nifedipine is in the range of 84%-89%. After ingestion of ADALAT CC tablets under fasting conditions, plasma concentrations peak at about 2.5-5 hours with a second small peak or shoulder evident at approximately 6-12 hours post dose. The elimination half-life of nifedipine administered as ADALAT CC is approximately 7 hours in contrast to the known 2 hour elimination half-life of nifedipine administered as an immediate release capsule.

When ADALAT CC is administered as multiples of 30 mg tablets over a dose range of 30 mg to 90 mg, the area under the curve (AUC) is dose proportional; however, the peak plasma concentration for the 90 mg dose given as 3×30 mg is 29% greater than predicted from the 30 mg and 60 mg doses.

Two 30 mg ADALAT CC tablets may be interchanged with a 60 mg ADALAT CC tablet. Three 30 mg ADALAT CC tablets, however, result in substantially higher C_{max} values than those after a single 90 mg ADALAT CC tablet. Three 30 mg tablets should, therefore, not be considered interchangeable with a 90 mg tablet.

Once daily dosing of ADALAT CC under fasting conditions results in decreased fluctuations in the plasma concentration of nifedipine compared to t.i.d. dosing with immediate release nifedipine capsules. The mean peak plasma concentration of nifedipine following a 90 mg ADALAT CC tablet, administered under fasting conditions, is approximately 115 ng/mL. When ADALAT CC is given immediately after a high fat meal in healthy volunteers, there is an average increase of 60% in the peak plasma nifedipine concentration, a prolongation in the time to peak concentration, but no significant change in the AUC. Plasma concentrations of nifedipine when ADALAT CC is taken after a fatty meal result in slightly lower peaks compared to the same daily dose of the immediate release formulation administered in three divided doses. This may be, in part, because ADALAT CC is less bioavailable than the immediate release formulation.

Nifedipine is extensively metabolized to highly water soluble, inactive metabolites accounting for 60% to 80% of the dose excreted in the urine. Only traces (less than 0.1% of the dose) of the unchanged form can be detected in the urine. The remainder is excreted in the feces in metabolized form, most likely as a result of biliary excretion.

No studies have been performed with ADALAT CC in patients with renal failure; however, significant alterations in the pharmacokinetics of nifedipine immediate release capsules have not been reported in patients undergoing hemodialysis or chronic ambulatory peritoneal dialysis. Since the absorption of nifedipine from ADALAT CC could be modified by renal disease, caution should be exercised in treating such patients.

Because hepatic biotransformation is the predominant route for the disposition of nifedipine, its pharmacokinetics may be altered in patients with chronic liver disease. ADALAT CC has not been studied in patients with hepatic disease; however, in patients with hepatic impairment (liver cirrhosis) nifedipine has a longer elimination half-life and higher bioavailability than in healthy volunteers.

The degree of protein binding of nifedipine is high (92%-98%). Protein binding may be greatly reduced in patients with renal or hepatic impairment.

After administration of ADALAT CC to healthy elderly men and women (age > 60 years), the mean C_{max} is 36% higher and the average plasma concentration is 70% greater than in younger patients.

Clinical Studies: ADALAT CC produced dose-related decreases in systolic and diastolic blood pressure as demonstrated in two double-blind, randomized, placebo-controlled trials in which over 350 patients were treated with ADALAT CC 30, 60 or 90mg once daily for 6 weeks. In the first study, ADALAT CC was given as monotherapy and in the second study, ADALAT CC was added to a beta-blocker in patients not controlled on a beta-blocker alone. The mean trough (24 hours post-dose) blood pressure results from these studies are shown below:

MEAN REDUCTIONS IN TROUGH SUPINE BLOOD PRESSURE (mmHg)
SYSTOLIC/DIASTOLIC

ADALAT CC DOSE	STUDY 1 N	MEAN TROUGH REDUCTION*
30 MG	60	5.3/2.9
60 MG	57	8.0/4.1
90 MG	55	12.5/8.1

ADALAT CC DOSE	STUDY 2 N	MEAN TROUGH REDUCTION*
30 MG	58	7.6/3.8
60 MG	63	10.1/5.3
90 MG	62	10.2/5.8

*Placebo response subtracted.

The trough/peak ratios estimated from 24 hour blood pressure monitoring ranged from 41%-78% for diastolic and 46%-91% for systolic blood pressure.

Hemodynamics: Like other slow-channel blockers, nifedipine exerts a negative inotropic effect on isolated myocardial tissue. This is rarely, if ever, seen in intact animals or man, probably because of reflex responses to its vasodilating effects. In man, nifedipine decreases peripheral vascular resistance which leads to a fall in systolic and diastolic pressures, usually minimal in normotensive volunteers (less than 5-10 mm Hg systolic), but sometimes larger. With ADALAT CC, these decreases in blood pressure are not accompanied by any significant change in heart rate. Hemodynamic studies of the immediate release nifedipine formulation in patients with normal ventricular function have generally found a small increase in cardiac index without major effects on ejection fraction, left ventricular end-diastolic pressure (LVEDP) or volume (LVEDV). In patients with impaired ventricular function, most acute studies have shown some increase in ejection fraction and reduction in left ventricular filling pressure.

Electrophysiologic Effects: Although, like other members of its class, nifedipine causes a slight depression of sinoatrial node function and atrioventricular conduction in isolated myocardial preparations, such effects have not been seen in studies in intact animals or in man. In formal electrophysiologic studies, predominantly in patients with normal conduction systems, nifedipine administered as the immediate release capsule has had no tendency to prolong atrioventricular conduction or sinus node recovery time, or to slow sinus rate.

INDICATION AND USAGE
ADALAT CC is indicated for the treatment of hypertension. It may be used alone or in combination with other antihypertensive agents.

CONTRAINDICATIONS
Known hypersensitivity to nifedipine.

WARNINGS
Excessive Hypotension: Although in most patients the hypotensive effect of nifedipine is modest and well tolerated, occasional patients have had excessive and poorly tolerated hypotension. These responses have usually occurred during initial titration or at the time of subsequent upward dosage adjustment, and may be more likely in patients using concomitant beta-blockers.

Severe hypotension and/or increased fluid volume requirements have been reported in patients who received immediate release capsules together with a beta-blocking agent and who underwent coronary artery bypass surgery using high dose fentanyl anesthesia. The interaction with high dose fentanyl appears to be due to the combination of nifedipine and a beta-blocker, but the possibility that it may occur with nifedipine alone, with low doses of fentanyl, in other surgical procedures, or with other narcotic analgesics cannot be ruled out. In nifedipine-treated patients where surgery using high dose fentanyl anesthesia is contemplated, the physician should be aware of these potential problems and, if the patient's condition permits, sufficient time (at least 36 hours) should be allowed for nifedipine to be washed out of the body prior to surgery.

Increased Angina and/or Myocardial Infarction: Rarely, patients, particularly those who have severe obstructive coronary artery disease, have developed well documented increased frequency, duration and/or severity of angina or acute myocardial infarction upon starting nifedipine or at the time of dosage increase. The mechanism of this effect is not established.

Beta-Blocker Withdrawal: When discontinuing a beta-blocker it is important to taper its dose, if possible, rather than stopping abruptly before beginning nifedipine. Patients recently withdrawn from beta blockers may develop a withdrawal syndrome with increased angina, probably related to increased sensitivity to catecholamines. Initiation of nifedipine treatment will not prevent this occurrence and on occasion has been reported to increase it.

Congestive Heart Failure: Rarely, patients (usually while receiving a beta-blocker) have developed heart failure after beginning nifedipine. Patients with tight aortic stenosis may be at greater risk for such an event, as the unloading effect of nifedipine would be expected to be of less benefit to these patients, owing to their fixed impedance to flow across the aortic valve.

PRECAUTIONS

General - Hypotension: Because nifedipine decreases peripheral vascular resistance, careful monitoring of blood pressure during the initial administration and titration of ADALAT CC is suggested. Close observation is especially recommended for patients already taking medications that are known to lower blood pressure (See WARNINGS).

Peripheral Edema: Mild to moderate peripheral edema occurs in a dose-dependent manner with ADALAT CC. The placebo subtracted rate is approximately 8% at 30 mg, 12% at 60 mg and 19% at 90 mg daily. This edema is a localized phenomenon, thought to be associated with vasodilation of dependent arterioles and small blood vessels and not due to left ventricular dysfunction or generalized fluid retention. With patients whose hypertension is complicated by congestive heart failure, care should be taken to differentiate this peripheral edema from the effects of increasing left ventricular dysfunction.

Information for Patients: ADALAT CC is an extended release tablet and should be swallowed whole and taken on an empty stomach. It should not be administered with food. Do not chew, divide or crush tablets.

Laboratory Tests: Rare, usually transient, but occasionally significant elevations of enzymes such as alkaline phosphatase, CPK, LDH, SGOT, and SGPT have been noted. The relationship to nifedipine therapy is uncertain in most cases, but probable in some. These laboratory abnormalities have rarely been associated with clinical symptoms; however, cholestasis with or without jaundice has been reported. A small increase ($<5\%$) in mean alkaline phosphatase was noted in patients treated with ADALAT CC. This was an isolated finding and it rarely resulted in values which fell outside the normal range. Rare instances of allergic hepatitis have been reported with nifedipine treatment. In controlled studies, ADALAT CC did not adversely affect serum uric acid, glucose, cholesterol or potassium.

Nifedipine, like other calcium channel blockers, decreases platelet aggregation *in vitro*. Limited clinical studies have demonstrated a moderate but statistically significant decrease in platelet aggregation and increase in bleeding time in some nifedipine patients. This is thought to be a function of inhibition of calcium transport across the platelet membrane. No clinical significance for these findings has been demonstrated.

Positive direct Coombs' test with or without hemolytic anemia has been reported but a causal relationship between nifedipine administration and positivity of this laboratory test, including hemolysis, could not be determined.

Although nifedipine has been used safely in patients with renal dysfunction and has been reported to exert a beneficial effect in certain cases, rare reversible elevations in BUN and serum creatinine have been reported in patients with pre-existing chronic renal insufficiency. The relationship to nifedipine therapy is uncertain in most cases but probable in some.

Drug Interactions: Beta-adrenergic blocking agents: (See WARNINGS).

ADALAT CC was well tolerated when administered in combination with a beta blocker in 187 hypertensive patients in a placebo-controlled clinical trial. However, there have been occasional literature reports suggesting that the combination of nifedipine and beta-adrenergic blocking drugs may increase the likelihood of congestive heart failure, severe hypotension, or exacerbation of angina in patients with cardiovascular disease.

Digitalis: Since there have been isolated reports of patients with elevated digoxin levels, and there is a possible interaction between digoxin and ADALAT CC, it is recommended that digoxin levels be monitored when initiating, adjusting, and discontinuing ADALAT CC to avoid possible over- or under-digitalization.

Coumarin Anticoagulants: There have been rare reports of increased prothrombin time in patients taking coumarin anticoagulants to whom nifedipine was administered. However, the relationship to nifedipine therapy is uncertain.

Quinidine: There have been rare reports of an interaction between quinidine and nifedipine (with a decreased plasma level of quinidine).

Cimetidine: Both the peak plasma level of nifedipine and the AUC may increase in the presence of cimetidine. Ranitidine produces smaller non-significant increases. This effect of cimetidine may be mediated by its known inhibition of hepatic cytochrome P-450, the enzyme system probably responsible for the first-pass metabolism of nifedipine. If nifedipine therapy is initiated in a patient currently receiving cimetidine, cautious titration is advised.

Carcinogenesis, Mutagenesis, Impairment of Fertility: Nifedipine was administered orally to rats for two years and was not shown to be carcinogenic. When given to rats prior to mating, nifedipine caused reduced fertility at a dose approximately 30 times the maximum recommended human dose. *In vivo* mutagenicity studies were negative.

Pregnancy: Pregnancy Category C. In rodents, rabbits and monkeys, nifedipine has been shown to have a variety of embryotoxic, placentotoxic and fetotoxic effects, including stunted fetuses (rats, mice and rabbits), digital anomalies (rats and rabbits), rib deformities (mice), cleft palate (mice), small placentas and underdeveloped chorionic villi (monkeys), embryonic and fetal deaths (rats, mice and rabbits), prolonged pregnancy (rats; not evaluated in other species), and decreased neonatal survival (rats; not evaluated in other species). On a mg/kg or mg/m^2 basis, some of the doses associated with these various effects are higher than the maximum recommended human dose and some are lower, but all are within an order of magnitude of it.

The digital anomalies seen in nifedipine-exposed rabbit pups are strikingly similar to those seen in pups exposed to phenytoin, and these are in turn similar to the phalangeal deformities that are the most common malformation seen in human children with *in utero* exposure to phenytoin.

There are no adequate and well-controlled studies in pregnant women. ADALAT CC should be used during pregnancy only if the potential benefit justifies the potential risk to the fetus.

Nursing Mothers: Nifedipine is excreted in human milk. Therefore, a decision should be made to discontinue nursing or to discontinue the drug, taking into account the importance of the drug to the mother.

ADVERSE EXPERIENCES

The incidence of adverse events during treatment with ADALAT CC in doses up to 90 mg daily were derived from multi-center placebo-controlled clinical trials in 370 hypertensive patients. Atenolol 50 mg once daily was used concomitantly in 187 of the 370 patients on ADALAT CC and in 64 of the 126 patients on placebo. All adverse events reported during ADALAT CC therapy were tabulated independently of their causal relationship to medication.

The most common adverse event reported with ADALAT® CC was peripheral edema. This was dose related and the frequency was 18% on ADALAT CC 30 mg daily, 22% on ADALAT CC 60 mg daily and 29% on ADALAT CC 90 mg daily versus 10% on placebo.

Other common adverse events reported in the above placebo-controlled trials include:

Adverse Event	ADALAT CC (%) (n=370)	PLACEBO (%) (n=126)
Headache	19	13
Flushing/heat sensation	4	0
Dizziness	4	2
Fatigue/asthenia	4	4
Nausea	2	1
Constipation	1	0

Where the frequency of adverse events with ADALAT CC and placebo is similar, causal relationship cannot be established.

The following adverse events were reported with an incidence of 3% or less in daily doses up to 90 mg:

Body as a Whole/Systemic: chest pain, leg pain
Central Nervous System: paresthesia, vertigo
Dermatologic: rash
Gastrointestinal: constipation
Musculoskeletal: leg cramps
Respiratory: epistaxis, rhinitis
Urogenital: impotence, urinary frequency

Other adverse events reported with an incidence of less than 1.0% were:

Body as a Whole/Systemic: cellulitis, chills, facial edema, neck pain, pelvic pain, pain
Cardiovascular: atrial fibrillation, bradycardia, cardiac arrest, extrasystole, hypotension, palpitations, phlebitis, postural hypotension, tachycardia, cutaneous angiectases
Central Nervous System: anxiety, confusion, decreased libido, depression, hypertonia, insomnia, somnolence
Dermatologic: pruritus, sweating
Gastrointestinal: abdominal pain, diarrhea, dry mouth, dyspepsia, esophagitis, flatulence, gastrointestinal hemorrhage, vomiting
Hematologic: lymphadenopathy
Metabolic: gout, weight loss
Musculoskeletal: arthralgia, arthritis, myalgia
Respiratory: dyspnea, increased cough, rales, pharyngitis
Special Senses: abnormal vision, amblyopia, conjunctivitis, diplopia, tinnitus
Urogenital/Reproductive: kidney calculus, nocturia, breast engorgement

The following adverse events have been reported rarely in patients given nifedipine in other formulations: allergenic hepatitis, alopecia, anemia, arthritis with ANA (+), depression, erythromelalgia, exfoliative dermatitis, fever, gingival hyperplasia, gynecomastia, leukopenia, mood changes, muscle cramps, nervousness, paranoid syndrome, purpura, shakiness, sleep disturbances, syncope, taste perversion, thrombocytopenin, transient blindness at the peak plasma level, tremor and urticaria.

OVERDOSAGE

Experience with nifedipine overdosage is limited. Generally, overdosage with nifedipine leading to pronounced hypotension calls for active cardiovascular support including monitoring of cardiovascular and respiratory function, elevation of extremities, judicious use of calcium infusion, pressor agents and fluids. Clearance of nifedipine would be expected to be prolonged in patients with impaired liver function. Since nifedipine is highly protein bound, dialysis is not likely to be of any benefit; however, plasmapheresis may be beneficial.

There has been one reported case of massive overdosage with tablets of another extended release formulation of nifedipine. The main effects of ingestion of approximately 4800 mg of nifedipine in a young man attempting suicide as a result of cocaine-induced depression was initial dizziness, palpitations, flushing, and nervousness. Within several hours of ingestion, nausea, vomiting, and generalized edema developed. No significant hypotension was apparent at presentation, 18 hours post ingestion. Blood chemistry abnormalities consisted of a mild, transient elevation of serum creatinine, and modest elevations of LDH and CPK, but normal SGOT. Vital signs remained stable, no electrocardiographic abnormalities were noted and renal function returned to normal within 24 to 48 hours with routine supportive measures alone. No prolonged sequelae were observed.

The effect of a single 900 mg ingestion of nifedipine capsules in a depressed anginal patient on tricyclic antidepressants was loss of consciousness within 30 minutes of ingestion, and profound hypotension, which responded to calcium infusion, pressor agents, and fluid replacement. A variety of ECG abnormalities were seen in this patient with a history of bundle branch block, including sinus bradycardia and varying degrees of AV block. These dictated the prophylactic placement of a temporary ventricular pacemaker, but otherwise resolved spontaneously. Significant hyperglycemia was seen initially in this patient, but plasma glucose levels rapidly normalized without further treatment.

A young hypertensive patient with advanced renal failure ingested 280 mg of nifedipine capsules at one time, with resulting marked hypotension responding to calcium infusion and fluids. No AV conduction abnormalities, arrhythmias, or pronounced changes in heart rate were noted, nor was there any further deterioration in renal function.

DOSAGE AND ADMINISTRATION

Dosage should be adjusted according to each patient's needs. It is recommended that ADALAT CC be administered orally once daily on an empty stomach. ADALAT CC is an extended release dosage form and tablets should be swallowed whole, not bitten or divided. In general, titration should proceed over a 7-14 day period starting with 30 mg once daily. Upward titration should be based on therapeutic efficacy and safety. The usual maintenance dose is 30 mg to 60 mg once daily. Titration to doses above 90 mg daily is not recommended.

If discontinuation of ADALAT CC is necessary, sound clinical practice suggests that the dosage should be decreased gradually with close physician supervision.

Care should be taken when dispensing ADALAT CC to assure that the extended release dosage form has been prescribed.

HOW SUPPLIED

ADALAT CC extended release tablets are supplied as 30 mg, 60 mg, and 90 mg round film coated tablets. The different strengths can be identified as follows:

Strength	Color	Markings
30 mg	Pink	30 on one side and ADALAT CC on the other side
60 mg	Salmon	60 on one side and ADALAT CC on the other side
90 mg	Dark Red	90 on one side and ADALAT CC on the other side

ADALAT® CC Tablets are supplied in:

	Strength	NDC Code
Bottles of 100	30 mg	0026-8841-51
	60 mg	0026-8851-51
	90 mg	0026-8861-51
Unit Dose Packages of 100	30 mg	0026-8841-48
	60 mg	0026-8851-48
	90 mg	0026-8861-48

The tablets should be protected from light and moisture and stored below 86°F (30°C). Dispense in tight, light-resistant containers.

Bayer

Pharmaceutical Division

Distributed by:

Bayer Corporation
Pharmaceutical Division
400 Morgan Lane
West Haven, CT 06516 USA
Made in Germany

PZ500005   3/95   © 1995 Bayer Corporation   4755